BRUMFIEL

THE INDIANS
of Manhattan Island and Vicinity

By ALANSON SKINNER

SIXTH EDITION

SCIENCE GUIDE No. 41

The American Museum of Natural History

New York, N. Y.

1947

A MAHIKAN INDIAN CHIEF FROM THE HUDSON RIVER BELOW ALBANY

Note his warclub, the shape of which is common in his region, the thunderbirds painted or tattooed on his face, and his belt embroidered with dyed deer's hair. His totem, the Tortoise, is at his feet. This man and the three Mohawk Chiefs shown following formed a party which visited England in 1709.

From an engraving in the possession of the New York Historical Society.

THE INDIANS OF MANHATTAN ISLAND AND VICINITY

By Alanson Skinner

INTRODUCTION

THERE is no subject which makes a more forceful appeal to the student, the historian, or even the general reader, than that of the native inhabitants of what is now Greater New York; yet there is no subject upon which it is more difficult to obtain information, for our Colonial ancestors have left us but few accounts of their observations, and these are in tomes that are rare and difficult of access.

The aborigines themselves have so nearly passed into oblivion, that no help can be obtained from their scattered and degenerate remnants in exile in the west, so that we must turn to two sources for our knowledge: the writings of the first white settlers, already mentioned, and the archaeological remains, the imperishable objects of stone, clay, bone and antler, which the vanished red men have left behind them on their ancient dwelling places.

The writings of the Colonists tell us that in appearance the Manhattan and their neighbors were tall and well-built, with black hair and eyes and not unpleasing faces. Their disposition is noted as mild, except when aroused, when they are said to have been very greedy of vengeance.

The men shaved their heads, or rather burned off their hair with hot stones, leaving often a standing roach of stiff black hair two or three inches high and as many broad, running from the forehead to the nape of the neck, and the lock which hung from the crown was generally allowed to grow much longer. This was the famous *scalplock*, which the warrior cultivated in defiance of the enemy, who might take it if he could. Sometimes they wore a roach of red dyed deer hair, exactly similar to those worn by the Sauk, Fox, Menomini, and other tribes of the Central West. Our Indians *did not* wear the feather war-bonnet so characteristic of the Sioux and other tribes of the Great Plains, and which is now always placed upon the Indians in the conventional drawings picturing the sale of Manhattan Island.

3

A MOHAWK CHIEF FROM THE MOHAWK VALLEY

Observe his tattooing and his belt embroidered with dyed deer's hair. His totem, the Bear, is shown at his side.

From an engraving in the possession of the New York Historical Society.

The Manhattan and their neighbors, unlike the Indians west and north of them, wore no shirts nor coats. Instead, they covered the upper parts of their bodies with robes made of dressed deerskin, or wolf, wildcat, or bear fur, or of the shimmering feathers of the wild turkey, neatly attached to a netted fabric. So closely and carefully were these feathers applied that they are said to have shed the rain.

The men also wore loin cloths or breechclouts of dressed leather, and leggings and moccasins of the same material. The moccasins of all the Indian tribes east of the Mississippi had one point in common, they were soft-soled, but west of the Mississippi region the tribes of the prairies used hard flat soles of rawhide for their shoes.

In addition to this costume, the warriors wore necklaces of dyed deer hair, of native copper or shell beads, or of wampum; and often they hung over their chests pendants of stone or gorgets, such as are still to be found occasionally upon the sites of their old camps. They also painted their faces with various pigments, especially red and black, which they obtained from limonite and graphite fragments. To this day one may find in the débris of an abandoned Indian village bits of these paint stones showing the striated markings of the stone scrapers with which the color was removed for use. The Manhattan, being a part of the Delaware tribe, an important group of the Algonkin stock, probably followed the ancient Delaware custom of tattooing their bodies, with designs representing their dreams and warlike exploits.

Old paintings of the Delaware show us that they wore their knives, and even their tobacco pipes and pouches, suspended from their necks. The reason for wearing their knives in this position, old Indians of some of the central western tribes declare, was so that they could be more readily seized at a moment's notice. Besides his deerskin tobacco pouch with its dyed hair and porcupine quill embroidery and leather fringe, each warrior carried a warclub, carved of wood, with a ball-shaped head set at right angles from the handle, and a six-foot bow and a quiver containing flint, bone, or antler-tipped arrows.

The women were differently clothed from the men. They often wore their hair in a braid, over which they drew a "square cap" ornamented with wampum. Presumably this hair dress was similar to that used by the Winnebago and Sauk and Fox women of the middle west, examples of which may be found in the cases in the Eastern Woodland Hall under the various tribal designations.

The women, like the men, were naked to the waist, save for the robe, which was shifted from side to side, according to whence the coldest wind

5

A MOHAWK CHIEF FROM THE MOHAWK VALLEY

His totem was the Wolf, which is shown beside him.

From an engraving in the possession of the New York Historical Society.

blew. They wore, however, knee leggings instead of the hip length style of the warriors, and wrapped about their waists a single square piece of fringed leather, which was open at one side. Sometimes these skirts were not made of leather, but instead were of cloth woven from Indian hemp, such as was also used to make bags. The women covered their gala costumes with wampum beads, and quill or hair embroidery, so that some of the old chronicles declare that a dress of this sort was often worth "above 300 guilders." Of course the women, like the men, protected their feet with dainty soft-soled moccasins.

The houses or wigwams of the Manhattan and their neighbors were never the conical shaped, leather-covered, painted tipis so often shown in illustrations. Lodges of that type were found only in the Great Plains area, and northward up the Mackenzie River and thence eastward about Hudson Bay and Labrador. The Manhattan lodges were of bark, and they and the other local tribes commonly built either square or semi-globular houses of poles arched over and set in the ground, covered with bark, mats made of rushes, with cornhusks, or sedge grass. Such houses looked very much like wooden bowls turned upside down. In the center of each wigwam a hole was dug in the earthen floor to hold the fire so that the sparks might not fly up and ignite the dry walls of the lodge.

In such fire holes, marking the sites of abandoned Indian houses, archaeologists may still find fire-cracked stones, wood ashes, the split bones of deer and other animals broken open to extract the marrow, oyster shells, fragments of earthen kettles, stone and bone implements, and all the discarded débris of the household utensils which were thrown away by their departed owners. Sometimes in such a place whole articles are found, hidden there perhaps during a sudden attack and never recovered by the owner. There too, in winter, when the frozen ground outside made digging impossible, the bodies of the dead were sometimes buried in the useful fireplace, and the lodge either destroyed or set up elsewhere. In proof of this skeletons have often been found in these forgotten fireplaces.

The interior furnishing of a round lodge was simple enough. A bench ran all around the inside of the wall, and on this the inhabitants both sat and slept. Poles swung horizontally from the roof supported strings of braided corn, baskets or bags of food, and other paraphernalia. A hole was left in the roof, directly over the hearth, for the smoke to escape.

Another kind of house, and one that was probably used most frequently in the summer, was a square lodge, made of poles and bark, with a pointed or rounded roof in which a long slot was left at the ridge for the escape of

7

TEE YEE NEEN HO GA Row, Emperour of the Six Nations.

A MOHAWK CHIEF FROM THE MOHAWK VALLEY

Note the wampum belt. His totem, the Wolf, is shown beside him.
From an engraving in the possession of the New York Historical Society.

smoke. Such a house was commonly occupied by a number of related families, and corresponded in many ways with the long tenements of the Iroquois. None of the houses and few of the villages of the local Indians were ever defended by palisades or trenches.

We are told by the old writers, and archaeological investigation confirms them, that the household utensils of the Indians were pottery vessels, nearly always, curiously enough, made with a pointed bottom, so that they had to be propped up with stones when in use, calabashes or gourds for water, spoons of shell and wood, wooden bowls laboriously made by burning and scraping knots or burls of trees, and bone awls and other tools.

The Indians derived their livelihood by farming a little, for they raised corn, beans, pumpkins, squashes, melons, and tobacco; but mostly by fishing, oystering, and clam gathering. They also were good hunters, as the bones of various animals, so common on their old kitchen refuse heaps, abundantly prove. However, from the vast heaps of oyster, clam, mussel, and other marine shells, that may be found scattered about the old Indian camping grounds, it is obvious that the sea furnished most of their food.

They caught fish in seines and gill nets, by harpooning, and by shooting with the bow and arrow; they killed deer and other game with the bow and arrow, often hunting in large companies. This was, with the waging of war, the duty of the men; the women tended the fields and probably built and owned the lodges.

In their fishing, and for traveling by water, our Indians used canoes, sometimes made from heavy elmbark but more often hollowed out of logs. Roger Williams says of the Narragansett and their neighbors:

Obs.: Mishoon, an Indian Boat, or Canow made of a Pine or Oake, or Chestnut-trees I have seene a Native goe into the woods with his hatchet carrying onely a Basket and Corne with him, and stones to strike fire when he had felled his tree (being a Chestnut) he made him a little House or shed of the bark of it, he puts fire and followes the burning of it with fire, in the midst in many places: his corne he boyles and hath the Brook by him and sometimes angles for a little fish: but so hee continues burning and hewing until he hath within ten or twelve dayes (lying there at his work alone) finished, and (getting hands), launched his boate with which afterward hee ventures out to fish in the Ocean.

* * * * * * *

Obs. Their owne reason hath taught them, to pull off a Coat or two and set it up on a small pole, with which they will saile before a wind ten, or twenty mile, &c.

* * * * * * *

9

Obs. It is wonderfull to see how they will venture in those Canoes, and how (being oft overset as I have myselfe been with them) they will swim a mile, yea two or more safe to Land: I having been necessitated to passe Waters diverse times: with them, it hath pleased God to make them many times the instruments of my preservation, and when sometimes in great danger I have questioned safety, they have said to me: Feare not, if we be overset I will carry you safe to Land.[1]

The NEW YORK TIMES for July 16, 1906, writes:

Cherry Hill was the centre of an excited crowd all day yesterday when the news got about that some workmen dug up an old Indian canoe in an excavation at the corner of Cherry and Oliver Streets.

Men, women, and boys and girls flocked to the spot and so blocked the streets that the police of the Oak Street Station had to be sent there to keep order.

The lower part of Oliver Street is made ground, for in the old days the waters of the East River used to wash above the Cherry Street line.

Workmen from the New York Edison Company had made an excavation about eight feet deep when they came to what seemed to be a big log near the bottom. They dug around this and disclosed to view what the police and all others who viewed it said was half of an Indian canoe. Then the workmen, who don't take much interest in anything pertaining to the American Indian, promptly got an axe and chopped away until they got out the timber in sight, leaving the other half still buried in the mud.

In doing this they split the canoe into three pieces, and followed by an admiring crowd, it was carried to the corner of Frankfort and Pearl Streets, and deposited on a pile of dirt under the Franklin Square elevated station, where the night watchman could keep his eye on it until today, when the workmen expect to get the other half and piece the canoe together.

It is supposed that the canoe was lying in the mud a hundred years ago or more, when the river front was filled in to make more land.

The part saved is about 7 feet long and 3 feet wide, and 14 inches deep, and tapers to an abrupt and rounded end, which is sharp, somewhat like the Indian canoes of the Western Indian. The whole was hewn from a solid log of white pine about fourteen feet long.

PART OF A DUGOUT CANOE

Found at Cherry St., New York. The only known fragment of a canoe used by the Indians of Manhattan.

[1]Collection of the Rhode Island Historical Society, vol. 1, pp. 98-99, Providence, 1827.

The Indian children, shortly after birth, were bound to a stiff board, which served as a cradle, and there they were kept until they were able to walk and run about. This served the double purpose of supporting their backs and also of keeping them out of mischief.

The religion of the Manhattan and their neighbors was a nature worship, pure and simple. They believed that there were deities who dwelt in the four quarters of the compass, that the sun and moon, the thunder and the winds were various supernatural beings. That these were all controlled by a supreme god whom they called "Kickeron," or "Kickerom," was their conviction. They thought that the earth was populated by the descendants of a woman who fell from the sky and who would have been lost in the sea, save that a gigantic tortoise which afterwards became the earth, caught her on his back. They were also in fear of a terrible evil power, a horned snake, to whom they made sacrifices by burying objects in the ground in its name.

The Manhattan and their neighbors also believed in a future existence, placing their Elysian fields in the southwestern skies, where they believed the souls of their dead journeyed. It was for this reason that they placed food and implements in their graves with the bodies, so that the wandering soul might lack nothing necessary to its comfort on the trip.

The religion of the Indians was marked by periodic ceremonies, one of which has come down to the present day among the modern remnants of the Shinnecock of Long Island and the Mohegan of Connecticut. This is the "June Meeting" which was formerly a ceremony held for the green corn. The Delaware in Oklahoma and Canada still perform a number of other annual ceremonies.

The old writers tell us that each Indian had some such name as "Buck's Horn," "Wildcat," or "Rattlesnake," and that when he died it was considered sacrilegious ever to mention his name again. It is also known that polygamy was practised by the local Indians.

The Archaeological Exhibits.

So much for the ethnology of the Manhattan and their neighbors. Let us now turn to their archaeology as set forth by the specimens on view in the entrance of the Woodland Hall.

On entering the Eastern Woodland Indian Hall the visitor will find that the first table sections are devoted to an exhibition, as comprehensive as possible, showing the life of the natives in prehistoric times by means of

INWODD ROCK-SHELTER, MANHATTAN

FINCH'S ROCK HOUSE

specimens obtained from the ancient village and camp sites. Here may be seen remains of the various animals, fish, and shell-fish upon which the Indians depended for subsistence; fragments of nuts, corn, roots, and other food products, preserved by charring, and obtained from ancient fireplaces; and such implements as arrow points of antler and stone, net-sinkers of stone, and stone hoes for tilling the field, all illustrative of primitive methods of hunting and agriculture. Implements exhibited in the same case show the preparation of animal and vegetable food with primitive utensils, while close by are tools used by the Indians in preparing skins. The manufactures of the Indians are illustrated in the immediately adjacent section.

A progressive series of implements shows the making of an arrow point from a simple quartz pebble such as might be picked up anywhere on the shore, with the various stages leading to the finished point; the tools employed are also exhibited. Implements of stone for pecking, grooving, and polishing; hatchets and axes; pottery fragments, and household utensils, such as hammers, axes, adzes, and gouges, will be found at hand.

In the upright cases there is an exhibit from Manhattan Island, made up of specimens principally collected by Messrs. Alexander C. Chenoweth, W. L. Calver, and R. P. Bolton, in the rock-shelters and village sites at Inwood, showing as fully as possible the life of the pre-historic Manhattan Indians.

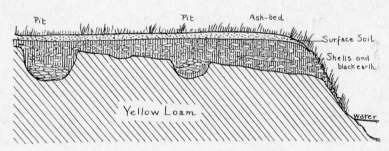

DIAGRAM OF A TYPICAL SHELL DEPOSIT

In another table case are to be seen implements and remains from the shell-heaps marking a long-forgotten Indian village at Shinnecock Hills, Long Island. This exhibit, which is one of the most complete of its kind, gives a rather adequate picture of the ancient life of these people and is especially valuable for the number and variety of primitive manufactures shown. One of the most interesting of the sections demonstrates, by means of a series of specimens, the primitive methods of cutting bone and antler employed by these Indians. Bone was cut by notching or grooving it with a stone knife or flake, and then breaking it at the groove. Antler was worked in the same way, but it is very probable that the Indians boiled antler in order to make it more pliable and easily cut.

From the appearance of pottery fragments now to be found on the sites of the ancient Indian villages of this vicinity and the methods of modern Indian pottery makers, we may safely conclude that most, if not all, of the earthenware manufactured in this locality was made by the coil process, which consisted of the following steps: The Indians first secured clay of a suitable quality, which was mixed with pounded shell or stones to make it tougher and more durable. It was then worked into long rolls, and the Indians, beginning at the bottom, worked the pot up by adding coil after coil, blending or smoothing the coils with a smooth stone until they did not show from either the interior or exterior surface. When the pot was completed, it was decorated by stamping or incising designs about the exterior of the rim.

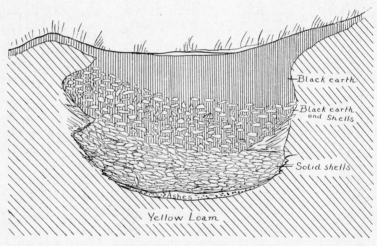

CROSS SECTION OF A SHELL PIT

The upright case at the end contains an exhibit from the remnants of the Algonkin and Iroquois Indians of New York State and New England, while a map showing the location of most of the Indian villages of Greater New York and vicinity and an actual section of a typical shell-heap, as well as photographs and labels describing the opening and excavation of the sites, are near at hand. Specimens typical of those found in the shell-heap are also exhibited.

Of all the traces left by the aborigines along the New York seacoast, the most abundant and familiar are the shell-heaps. These are beds of refuse marking the sites of ancient villages, camps, and isolated wigwams. Wherever the fresh water joins the salt, especially where open water for fishing and a spring for drinking come together in happy combination, there is generally to be found some such evidence of Indian occupation.

The typical "shell-heap" is not a heap at all, for leaf mold, the wash from neighboring high ground, and often cultivation have generally made it level with its surroundings (page 14). Very often, unless the land be plowed, no shells whatever show on the surface, and the only way of finding out the condition of things below the sod is to test with a spade or a crowbar. If shells are present, their crunching soon gives notice of the fact. Sometimes shell-heaps have been located by shells thrown from animal burrows, or washed out by the rain, or in banks broken down by the surf. Some have been found fronting on the open Sound, but such cases are rare. These deposits consist of large quantities of decayed oyster, clam, and other marine shells mixed with stained earth, with ashes, charcoal, and fire-cracked stones to mark the spots where ancient camp fires blazed. Among the shells are usually scattered antler of deer, bones of animals, fishes, and birds, quantities of pottery fragments, and broken implements; in short, the imperishable part of the camp refuse left by the Indians. Now and then, perfect implements, and ornaments that had been carelessly lost in the rubbish or hidden for safe-keeping are discovered.

Shell-heaps vary from a few inches to four feet in depth, and in area from a few square yards to several acres—all depending on the length of time the settlement was occupied and the number of dwellings comprising it. Deep shell-heaps are often divided into layers, the lowest of which are, of course, the oldest. Under and near most of these deposits may be found scattered "pits" or fire holes, which are bowl-shaped depressions in the ground filled with layers of stained earth, shells, and other refuse, with an occasional layer of ashes. Some pits are as large as ten feet wide by six feet deep, but the average is four feet deep by three feet wide. It is supposed that they were used as ovens or steaming holes and afterwards filled up with refuse. Some contain human skeletons, which may have been interred in them during the winter season when grave digging was impossible. These pits generally contain more of interest than the ordinary shell-heap. The closely packed regular masses of shells form a covering which tends to preserve

15

bone implements, charred corn, and such perishable articles from decay in a way that the looser shells of the general layers fail to do.

Shell-heaps, while abundant along the seacoast, are seldom found inland, except on salt creeks or other streams having access to salt water. They may be seen all along the east shore of the Hudson River at more or less frequent intervals as far up as Peekskill; on Croton Point and between Nyack and Hook Mountain on the west shore they attain considerable size. There are a few small deposits, however, composed mainly of fresh water clams (Unio) situated on fresh water lakes in the interior of Westchester

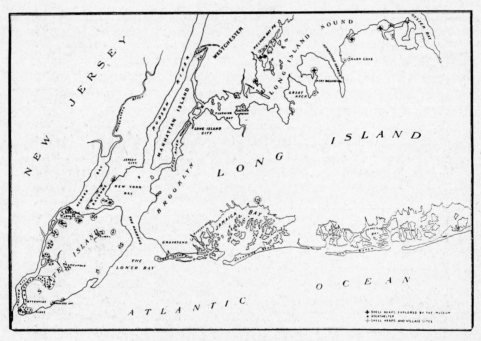

MAP GIVING THE LOCATIONS OF SHELL DEPOSITS

Those marked + have been explored by the Museum

County. There are many shell-heaps on Staten Island. Shell-heaps occur or did occur on Constable Hook, New Jersey, and at intervals between there and Jersey City along the western shore of New York Bay. The accompanying map gives the location of the important known shell deposits in the vicinity of New York City.

Besides the shell-heaps, the ancient cemeteries of the Indians hold much of interest to the archaeologist.

Although most of the natives in the vicinity of Greater New York did not place objects in the graves with their dead, some graves at Burial Ridge, Tottenville, Staten Island, when opened for the Museum in 1895, were found to contain a great many interesting and valuable remains. With the skeleton of a child there was a great deposit of utensils, both finished and unfinished ornaments, such as beads, pendants, and the like, a stone pipe,

INDIAN SKELETONS PIERCED BY ARROW POINTS, TOTTENVILLE, STATEN ISLAND

and a number of other objects, while not far away the skeletons of three Indian warriors were exhumed, in and among whose bones there were found, as shown in the cases devoted to the archaeology of Staten Island, twenty-three arrow points of stone, antler, and bone.

17

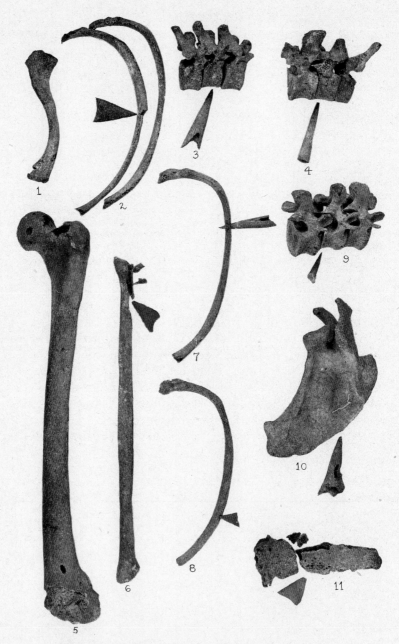

BONES PUNCTURED BY ARROW POINTS, FROM SKELETONS
FOUND ON STATEN ISLAND

This is an exhibit which excellently indicates the use of the bow in Indian warfare. In the first skeleton, it was found that two arrow points of antler and one of bone had pierced the body and lodged near the spinal column. Another point of argillite had been driven between two ribs, cutting a notch in each. A bone arrow point had struck the shoulder and was resting against the scapula. Among the bones of the right hand, an arrow point of antler was discovered, and there was a similar one near the left hand. Another antler point was lying in the sand just beneath the body and had, no doubt, dropped from it when the flesh wasted away. The most interesting wound of all was one where an antler-tipped arrow had plowed through one side of the body and fully one-third of the point had passed through one of the ribs, making a hole, in which it remained. The second warrior was also terribly injured. The left femur showed an elongated puncture near the lower end, probably made by an arrow point. Among the ribs was the tip of an antler point, and another of yellow jasper was among the ribs on the left side of the body. Three other points were among the bones. The third skeleton was likewise an example of old-time bow play. There was an antler point among the ribs of the left side. The end of one of the fibulæ was shattered by a stone arrow-head, and a second point had lodged between two ribs. Beneath the sternum was a flint point, and the right shoulder blade showed a fracture near the end, caused by a blow of some hand implement or an arrow. Near the base of the skull, the end of an antler arrow-head was discovered, broken perhaps by its impact with the occiput. Two bone points were near the lower bones of the left leg. A second point was found upon search among the left ribs; under the vertebræ was the base of another antler point, and two broken points were found beneath the body.

The positions in which several of the points were found certainly speak well for the great force which propelled them. The long bows of the local Indians must indeed have been formidable weapons. Taking into consideration the number of arrows which must have been imbedded in the bodies of the warriors, it is perhaps probable that the majority of the projectiles were driven into the victims at close range after death.

In a small square case will be found the model of a rock-shelter and typical objects found in such places. These rock-shelters, as the name implies, are protected spots in rocky ledges, which Indians once made more or less permanent places of abode. Many such shelters exist in the vicinity of New York, two or more having been discovered at Inwood, Manhattan. The most important rock-shelter so far discovered is the so-called Finch Rock

19

House reproduced in a model. The original is near Armonk, Westchester County, New York. One point of special interest is the fact that the Finch shelter contained two layers bearing relics separated by sand as shown in the drawing. As no pottery was found in the bottom layer, it has been inferred that we have here the remains of two different races of Indians, the older not yet advanced to the pottery-making stage. This conclusion, is, however, far from final, for the whole arrangement may be due to accident.

In the table cases opposite those devoted to the Algonkin some sections are used to show the life history of the Iroquois tribes of western New York, and the following section shows, as well as possible, the culture of the Five Nations and objects used by the Indians of New York State obtained from European traders after the advent of the settlers.

With the Iroquois exhibit is a special exhibit showing typical wampum beads, belts, and implements illustrating the prehistoric manufacture of wampum on Long Island.

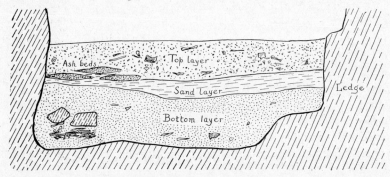

VERTICAL SECTION IN FINCH'S ROCK HOUSE,
ABOUT MIDWAY OF THE CAVE

TYPES OF INDIAN RELICS FOUND IN AND ABOUT NEW YORK CITY

HAVING now taken a general view of the exhibit, the visitor may be interested in a study of the several kinds of relics found in this locality. As these types are somewhat unlike those found in near-by regions, we conclude that the Indians formerly living here had habits and customs different from those of their neighbors. For want of a better name, these long-extinct tribes have been called collectively the New York Coastal Algonkin. The term Algonkin designates the language they spoke, while the adjectives define their habitat. Under the designation New York

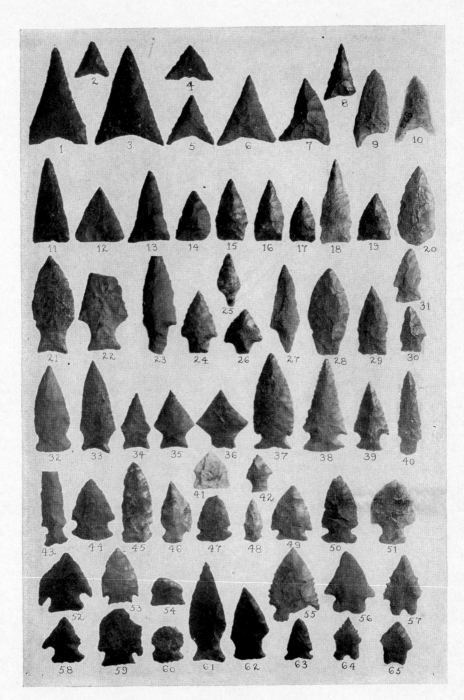

TYPES OF ARROW POINTS

Coastal Algonkin, the writer includes the tribes along the coast from Totten-ville, Staten Island, the extreme southern point of the state, to the Connecti-cut boundary on Long Island Sound, including to a certain extent the shores of New Jersey immediately adjacent to Staten and Manhattan Islands, the east bank of the Hudson River as far north as Yonkers, and the Western end of Long Island.

From the examination of the remains of the New York Coastal Algon-kian area preserved in many collections, both public and private, it becomes obvious that the objects found may be roughly divided into three groups: articles of stone, articles of bone and antler, and articles of clay, shell, and metal. The first group is, from the imperishable nature of its representatives, naturally the largest and comprises a number of sub-groups to be briefly described and commented upon in this paper. Examples of this type will be found in the table cases previously mentioned. For the following descrip-tions and historical notes the author has largely drawn on Mr. James K. Finch's and his own contributions to Volume III of the "Anthropological Papers of the American Museum of Natural History" (New York, 1909).

Chipped Articles.

Arrow Points. Two general types of arrow points may be recognized: these are the stemmed, or notched, and the triangular forms. The former are by far the most abundant, and while these are usually made of the nearest local rock possessing the necessary conchoidal fracture, in some cases they are of material brought from a long distance. Specimens made of pink flint resembling stone from the Flint Ridge of Ohio, and of jasper found to the south of this region, have been recorded. Blunt arrow points are rare, the Indians probably preferring wooden arrows for this type. Many of the so-called "blunt points" found in collections appear to be scrapers made over from broken arrow points of a large size.

The triangular type has long been regarded by the local collectors of this vicinity as being the type used in war, the argument being that as it has no stem, it was necessarily but loosely fastened in its shaft and, if shot into the body, would be very liable to become detached and remain in the flesh if any attempt were made to withdraw it by tugging at the shaft. While it was no doubt perfectly possible to fasten a point of triangular shape to the shaft as firmly as a notched point, the discoveries of Mr. George H. Pepper at Tottenville, Staten Island, where twenty-three arrow points were found in and among the bones of three Indian skeletons, tend to strengthen this

KNIVES AND SCRAPERS

theory. While the majority of points found there were of bone or antler, all those made of stone were of this type; indeed, most of the bone points were also triangular in shape. However, it is well to bear in mind that arrow points of triangular type were used for every purpose by all the early Iroquois tribes of New York.

Spear Points and Knives. None of the early accounts of contemporary European writers seems to mention the use of spears (other than bone or antler-headed harpoons) by the Indians hereabouts, and it is probable that the larger arrow-point forms found were used as knives or cutting tools. They are usually notched or stemmed, rarely triangular, and occasionally round or oval. They vary in size, but it must be remembered that one tool may have had various uses, and that drills, knives, and scrapers may often have been combined in one implement.

Scrapers. Scrapers were probably used in dressing skins, in sharpening bone implements, wood-working, and for various other purposes. These are usually mere flint flakes chipped to an edge on one side. Nevertheless, notched and stemmed forms requiring some care in their making, do occur. Broken arrow points were occasionally chipped down to serve this purpose. A single serrated scraper has been found. These are very rare in both the Algonkian and Iroquois areas of New England and the Middle Atlantic States. One very large stemmed scraper, of a type more common in the far west, also comes from this locality.

Drills. These are usually chipped tools presenting an elongated narrow blade and a considerably swollen or expanded base, suitable for grasping in the hand. In some cases the base was absent and those were probably hafted in wood. Specimens with blades having a square or rectangular cross-section are very rare. The finding of cores left in half-drilled objects shows the use of a hollow drill, and it has been suggested that a hard hollow reed used with sand and water on a soft stone would produce this effect. To bear out this assertion, it has been reported that a half-drilled implement has been found outside this area on the upper Hudson in which the remains of the reed drill were found in the cavity left by its action.

ROUGH STONE ARTICLES.

Hammerstones. These vary from simple pebbles picked up and used in the rough, showing merely a battered edge or edges acquired by use, to the pitted forms. They are generally mere pebbles with a pit pecked on two opposite sides, perhaps to aid in grasping with the thumb and forefinger.

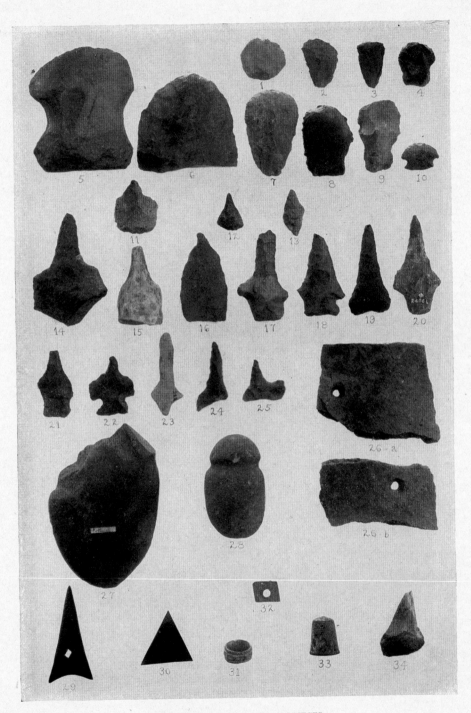

DRILLS, SCRAPERS AND OTHER OBJECTS

Some have battered edges, but many have not, suggesting, when round and regular, a use as gaming or "Chunké" stones, or as implements used only in pounding some rather soft substance. Hammerstones, pitted on one side only, and others with many pits on all sides, occur. These latter may have had some special use, and are not to be comfounded with the large, flat, slab-like stones having pits only on one side, found in other regions, and perhaps used as receptacles for holding nuts while cracking them. While these are common in the Iroquoian area, they are unknown here.

Large stones, single or double-pitted, resembling over-sized hammerstones, occur. These may have been used as anvils in chipping flint or for like purposes.

Grooved clubs or mauls, also showing use as hammers, are found. These are rare and are usually either rough pebbles, grooved for hafting, as in the case of the grooved axe, or grooved axes, the blades of which have become so battered, broken, and rounded by wear as to preclude their further use for chopping.

Net-Sinkers. On all sites near the water, either salt or fresh, net-sinkers show the prevalence of fishing. These are of two types. In one case a pebble is notched on opposite sides of either the long or broad axis; in the other, a groove is pecked around the entire pebble in the same manner. The latter type is comparatively scarce, as the former, being more easily and quickly made, was just as useful to the savage. The modern Cree and Ojibway, residing in the forests north of the Great Lakes, still use pebbles for this purpose, but those observed by the writer were not notched or worked in any way. Occassionally, sinkers notched on both axes are found in this region.

Hoes. These are usually ovoid implements, chipped from trap rock, sometimes notched to facilitate hafting, and sometimes not. They usually show a slight polish on the blade, caused by friction with the ground. This type of stone hoe is the form mentioned by early writers; but perhaps hoes of shell, bone, or tortoise shell, and wood were used also. None of these, however, are still in existence.

Hand Choppers. Pebbles chipped to an edge on one side, for use as hand choppers, occur. These are occasionally pitted on both sides.

Grooved Axes. For the purposes of this paper, the writer, while aware that many grooved axes are well made and polished, has decided to include them under the head of "Rough Stone Articles," as by far the greater majority of the grooved axes and celts from this region lack the polish and finish belonging to other articles later to be described. Grooved axes are of

TYPES OF STONE AXES AND CELTS

two sorts: *a*, those made of simple pebbles, merely modified by grooving and chipping or pecking an edge; and *b*, axes which have been pecked and worked all over and sometimes polished. The latter (*b*) may be said to include:

    1.   Groove encircling three sides of blade, one side flat.

    2.   Ridged groove encircling three sides of blade, one side flat.

    3.   Groove encircling three sides of blade, longitudinal groove on flat side.

    4.   Groove encircling three sides of blade, longitudinal groove on flat side and opposite.

HAFTED CELT FROM A POND AT THORNDALE, DUTCHESS CO., N. Y.
Length of celt 16.6 cm.

    5.   Groove encircling blade.

    6.   Ridged groove encircling blade.

A seventh type, having a double groove encircling the blade, may occur in this territory, but has never been reported. A specimen from the Hudson River region, just north of the area here dwelt upon, is in the Henry Booth

Collection in this Museum. While most worked stone axes have been pecked into shape, a few have been fashioned by chipping but these seem to be rare.

Grooved axes were hafted in various ways. During the summer of 1908, the Eastern Cree living in the vicinity of the southern end of Hudson Bay told the writer that their ancestors, who made and used such axes, hafted them by splitting a stick and setting the blade in it, then binding the handle together with deerskin (probably rawhide) above and below the split. No specimens of the grooved axe in the original haft seem now to be extant from any locality in the East. From the battered appearance of the butts of these axes, it may have been that they were sometimes used in lieu of mauls or hammers. It is possible that they may have been used in war. It is generally supposed that in cutting down trees, making dug-out canoes, and other kinds of wood-working, fire was used as an adjunct to the stone axe, the former being the active agent. The process of burning and charring having gone on sufficiently, the stone axe was used to remove the burned portion. However, some stone axes seem sharp enough to cut quite well without the aid of fire.

Celts. Ungrooved axes or hatchets, usually called celts, are frequent throughout this area; but are nowhere as abundant as the grooved axe, especially near the southern border of the region. The grooved axe seems to have been the typical cutting and chopping tool of the local Algonkin. The widespread idea that the celt was sometimes used unhafted as a skinning tool, has no historic proof, but may possibly have some foundation. The Cree of the southern Hudson Bay region use an edged tool of bone for this purpose, a fact which is somewhat suggestive, although the implement differs in shape from the celt. Celts with one side flat and the other beveled to an edge may have been used as adzes. From the worn and hammered appearance of the polls of some celts, it is possible that many of these implements were used as wedges in splitting wood, after constant manipulation in their chopping capacity had permanently dulled their edges.

The celts of this region are, as a general thing, poorly made, a pebble of suitable shape having an edge ground on it with little or no preliminary shaping. More rarely, however, they were carefully worked all over by pecking and polishing, as in the case of the grooved axe.

In type, aside from the general division of rough and worked celts, we may add that most celts in this region have slightly rounded polls, the bit broader than the butt, although some exceptions have been found. The forms are as follows: *a*, rough stone celts, pebbles with one end ground to an

29

edge, but otherwise scarcely worked; and *b*, worked stone celts, which include the following:

1. Wedge-shaped, poll narrower than bit, and angles rounded. Common.

2. Like number one, but with bit much broader than poll. Cross-section oval. Very rare.

3. Like number one, but one side flat, other beveled at one end to make a cutting edge.

4. Like number two, but with cutting edge flaring, broader than body. "Bell-mouthed type." Very rare.

North and west of this region we find the Iroquois territory, where most worked celts are angular, having almost invariably a rectangular cross-section and squared butt. Types 1 and 3 also occur, but the celt with the rectangular cross-section seems most typical of the Iroquoian region. Many small celts, made of flat fragments or chips of stone, are also found in this area, and these could scarcely have had a use as chopping tools.

In the Niagara watershed and extending eastward as far as the Genesee Valley, an angular adze-like form having a trapezoidal cross-section occurs. It is found principally in what was the territory of the Attiwandaronk, Kah-Kwah, or Neutral Nation (an Iroquoian tribe, early annihilated by the Five Nations). It also occurs as has been stated, on the sites of villages of the Iroquois proper, but is not abundant. South of the Iroquois in Central Pennsylvania, another form which does not occur in this region is the chipped celt, usually of flint or other hard stone. This form is, however, frequent in the country about the headwaters of the Delaware.

In the "American Anthropologist," Vol. 9, No. 2, p. 296, *et seq.*, Mr. C. C. Willoughby has figured and described the celts of the New England region with remarks on the methods of hafting employed. These seem to be two in number, and consist, in the case of the larger forms, of setting the blade through a hole in the end of a club-like handle, the butt or poll projecting on one side and the blade on the other as in one which was found in the muck of a pond bottom at Thorndale, Dutchess County, New York, a region once in the Mahikan territory. Smaller celts were set into a club-like handle, the butt resting in a hole or socket.

Adzes. These seem to be of two kinds, the first and most simple being celt-like, but flat on one side, the other side being beveled to an edge on one side. The second form differs in having a groove, which is not infrequently ridged. Occasionally, adzes with two parallel grooves occur. They were

30

BANNER STONES, GORGETS, AND AMULETS

probably hafted by taking a stick at one end of which projected a short arm at right angles with the shaft, laying the flat side of the blade against this arm and binding it on with sinew, thongs, or withes. The groove, of course, was of aid in securing the blade to the handle. Adzes of stone, hafted in this manner, have been obtained on the North Pacific Coast. The celt adze seems not uncommon, but the grooved adze is rare, neither form being nearly so abundant as in the New England region.

Gouges. The stone gouge is rare, and seems always to be a plain, single-bladed affair without the transverse grooves so frequently seen in New England specimens, and hereabouts is always easily distinguished from the adze. Less than half a dozen specimens have been seen by the writer from this entire area, although probably quite as much work in wood was done by the New York Coastal Algonkian as by the New England Indians.

Pestles. The long pestle occurs throughout the region of the Coastal Algonkin of New York, but is nowhere as abundant as in New England. They seem always to have been used with the wooden block mortar hereabouts, and are mentioned by the early writers as part of the household equipment of the natives. They do not seem to have been used by the Iroquois to the north and west of this area either in early or later times. The wooden pestle of dumb-bell shape seems to have been preferred by them. The latter is used by the Canadian Delaware and may have taken the place of the long stone pestle to a great extent in this region.

Mullers, Grinders, and Polishing Stones. These are frequent, and consist merely of rounded pebbles, shaped and worn by use, probably most often in crushing corn. They are mentioned by De Vries as being used by the Indians with a flat stone slab for grinding corn when traveling. Some seem to have been used for polishing stone implements, but it seems hard to draw the line, as the appearance gained from friction would be quite similar. Such mullers and their attendant slabs, used for preparing cornmeal have within a few years been collected in use among the Oneida Iroquois of New York, one specimen being in the American Museum collection.

Sinew Stones. These are pebbles showing grooves along the edges, popularly supposed to have been worn there by rubbing thongs and sinews across the edges to shape them. They occur generally, but are not common.

Stone Mortars. These are common, but rather local, some sites having none at all, and others a good many. One locality on Staten Island is

32

notable for the numbers found there, whereas they are rare elsewhere in that vicinity. They may be divided into the following types:

1. Portable mortar, hole on one side.
2. Portable mortar, hole on both sides (New Jersey type).
3. Portable slab mortar or metate, used on one or both sides.
4. Boulder mortar, one or more holes, immovable.

The first two types are the most abundant, the third is not uncommon, but the fourth is very rare, only one or two being reported. As above stated, De Vries claims that the portable mortars were used in bread-making while the Indians were traveling, but certainly the majority of those found are far too heavy for this purpose.

Pigments and Paint Cups. Fragments of pigments such as graphite and limonite, showing the marks of scratching with scrapers, are found. These have apparently supplied the material for painting. Worked geodes are common on many sites. These show traces of chipping in some instances and may have been paint cups. There is a tiny pestle-shaped pebble in the Museum collection from Westchester County, which is said to have been found with a geode of this type. The popular theory is that such geodes were used as "paint cups" and this seems probable.

Stone Plummets. These are very rare, in contrast to their abundance in the New England region. They consist usually of small worked egg-shaped stones, grooved at one end, probably for suspension. The writer has seen but one from this area. Their use is problematic.

Semilunar Knives. Knives of rubbed slate, similar in appearance to the ulu, or woman's knife of the Eskimo, are found, though rarely, in this region. While sometimes ascribed to Eskimo influence or contact, it is possible that this form (which occurs throughout New England), judging by its distribution, may have been native to the Eastern Algonkin also. The Eastern Cree still use knives of this type as scrapers. Like most other forms common in New England, it is less abundant in the southern part of this area.

Stone Beads. Various pebbles generally perforated naturally are to be found on some sites, and may or may not have been used as beads or pendants. On Staten Island, at Watchogue, Mr Isaiah Merrill once owned a number of square beads of pinkish steatite (?), all but one of which have been lost, and which he claims were found on his farm.

33

Gorgets. Two types of the gorget occur. These are the single-holed pendant form, which is the less abundant of the two, and the double-holed type. The latter is flat, rectangular in shape, and generally well polished. It usually has two perforations a short distance from the middle. The modern Lenapé of Canada claim to have used these as hair ornaments. Probably the two-holed variety is typical of the Algonkian peoples of this region; the single-holed form, on the other hand, is the most abundant on old Iroquoian sites. Specimens of the latter have been obtained in use among the Canadian Iroquois, and some of them are in the Museum collections.

Amulets. Certain problematic articles of the "bar" and even "bird amulet" type have been found, but these are probably exotic in origin and are not characteristic of the archæology of the region in question.

Banner Stones. These beautiful polished stone implements of unknown use may be divided into three great classes, with several sub-types as follows:

1. Notched banner stones.
2. Grooved banner stones.
   a. Groove on both sides.
   b. Groove on one side.
3. Perforated banner stones.
   a. Plain.
   b. Butterfly.

All three types seem equally abundant, but the notched banner stones appear to be the oldest form and occur under circumstances pointing to great relative antiquity. They are found, however, on the more recent sites as well. Both the notched and the grooved banner stones are usually more rough in appearance than the perforated type, and the writer has never seen a polished specimen of the first class. On the other hand, the grooved variety frequently exhibits the high degree of finish characteristic of the perforated forms. Banner stones grooved only on one side are less common than the other forms. While the latter class is generally made of slate, steatite, or some similar soft and easily worked material, the notched and grooved forms, especially the former, are often formed either from naturally-shaped pebbles or chipped roughly into shape. Implements, usually naturally-shaped stones with little working, without notches, grooves, or perforations but greatly resembling the notched and grooved banner stones in shape, are not infrequently found in aboriginal sites hereabouts

34

and may have served as banner stones. There seem to be neither records nor palusible theories as to their use.

Pipes. Stone pipes, invariably made of steatite, are very rare. Four types have been noted as follows:

1. Monitor or platform pipe, platform not projecting before the bowl.

2. Monitor or platform pipe, platform projecting before bowl, with or without tiny carved stem or mouthpiece. Of the latter, only one specimen is known.

3. Trumpet-shaped stone pipe.

4. Rectangular stone pipe, human face carved on front of bowl.

It may be remarked that more stone pipes have been reported from the Indian cemetery at Burial Ridge, Tottenville, Staten Island, than from all the rest of the area put together. The second and third types are represented by one specimen each from Burial Ridge and from nowhere else in this region. Four or five pipes of the first class have been found there as well. The last class is by a single specimen represented obtained by Mr. W. L. Calver at Inwood, Manhattan Island. Undoubtedly the clay pipe was the most common form used in this locality.

Steatite Vessels. These are not at all abundant, though occurring almost everywhere. They were doubtless all imported from New England, as there are no steatite quarries within the range of the New York Coastal Algonkin. The single form found is that common in the East, an oblong, fairly deep vessel with a lug, ear, or handle at each end. Occasionally, such vessels are ornamented by rude incisions along the rim.

ARTICLES OF CLAY.

Pottery Pipes are common everywhere. They are usually manufactured of a better quality of clay than that used for vessels, and bear fairly similar designs. They are susceptible of division into the following classes:

1. Straight tubular form, bowl expanding slightly.

2. Bowl much larger than stem, leaving it at an angle of forty-five degrees. Stem round.

3. Same as number 2, but stem angular and much flattened.

4. Effigy pipes (represented by a human head apparently broken from a pipe bowl, obtained by Mr. M. R. Harrington at Port Washington, Long Island.)

The straight pipe seems to have been obtained only on Staten Island, on the north shore, in the region occupied by the Hackensack. While nowhere as abundant as upon the Iroquoian sites of central and western New York, the clay pipe is rather common and is a prominent feature in the coast culture of New York. It is more abundant perhaps in the southern part of the area, but this may well be due to the fact that data from this region are more easily accessible. The triangular-stemmed "trumper" pipe so common on the Iroquoian sites is unknown in this region.

POTTERY VESSELS.

The pottery of this region may all be considered as being either the native Algonkian in type or showing Iroquoian influence with a third and intermediate variety. Algonkian vessels may be divided into the following groups according to shape:

1. Conical, pointed bottom, slightly swollen sides, circumference largest at the mouth,—the typical Algonkian pot of this area. Fig. a.

2. Like number 1, but much rounder and broader, Fig. b.

3. Bottom pointed, sides slightly swollen, neck slightly constricted, Fig. c.

4. Identical with number 2, except that just below the beginning of the neck, occur small raised lugs, ears, or handles. This is rare from this area, Fig. d.

5. Rounded bottom, somewhat constricted neck, lip sometimes flaring, or even turning down and back, Fig. e.

The intermediate types are as follows:

6. Rounded bottom, constricted neck, narrow raised rim or collar, Fig. f.

7. Like number 6, but with sides more elongated and bottom more oval than round, heavier collar, generally notched angle, with or without a series of small humps or projections at intervals, Fig. g.

The Iroquoian types are as follows:

8. Mouth rounded, collar or rim heavy, with humps or peaks at intervals, angle notched, neck constricted and bottom rounded, can stand by itself, an unknown feature in local Algonkian vessels, Fig. h.

9. Same as number 7, but with mouth square, and humps at every angle. Much less common than in the preceding, Fig. i.

In size, the vessels range from small toy-like pots to jars of very large capacity. In general they appear to have been made by the coil process, and are tempered with pounded stone or fine gravel, mica or burned or pounded shell. Sherds showing tempering by fiber or some other sub-stance that disappeared in firing are found rarely. When vessels were cracked or broken, a series of holes was bored opposite each other on either side of the break and the parts laced together, rendering the vessel capable of storing dry objects, at least.

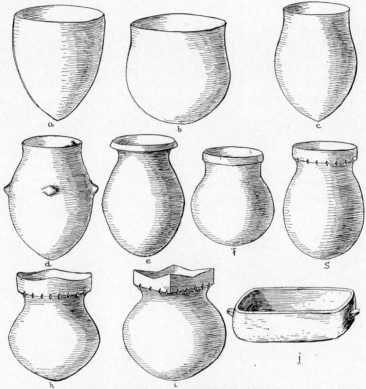

POTTERY FORMS OF THE CENTRAL ALGONKIN

Life forms are exceedingly rare in local ceramic art. From Manhattan Island and Van Cortlandt Park, there come a number of specimens showing incised human (?) faces. This is not an uncommon form on Iroquoian sites in Central and Western New York. On the Bowman's Brook site at Mariner's Harbor, Staten Island, fragments of a typically Algonkian pot were obtained which bore at intervals rude raised faces. With the sole exception of a rather well-modeled clay face, apparently, broken from the bowl of a pipe found at Port Washington, Long Island by Mr. M. R. Harrington, this brief statement concludes the list of pottery life forms reported from this area, although others may yet be found here, since some interesting objects have been collected in immediately adjacent territory.

The forms of decoration consist of stamping with a stamp, roulette, or paddle, and incising. Occasionally, but very rarely, stucco work occurs. Under stamping we can enumerate the following processes:

1. Impression with the rounded end of a stick (rare).
2. Impression with the end of a quill, or hollow reed, leaving a circular depression with a tiny lump or nipple (rare) in the center.
3. Impression with a section of a hollow reed, making a stamped circle (rare).
4. Impression with finger nail (doubtful, but perhaps used on some sherds from Manhattan Island).
5. Impression of the edge of a scallop shell.
6. Impression with a carved bone, antler, or wooden stamp.
7. Impression of a cord, wrapped stick.
8. Impression with roulette.

Under the head of decoration by incision we can enumerate the following:

9. Incised decoration, probably made with a stick.
10. Incised decoration possibly made with a flint object (only one specimen at hand).

The paddle was frequently used to finish the sides and bottom of the pot by imparting an appearance of pressure with fabric when the clay was wet.

11. Stucco. Occasionally, ridges of clay placed on the rim for ornament appear to have been added after the shaping of the vessel.

Ornamentation is usually external, and vessels, either Algonkian or Iroquoian, are rarely ornamented below the rim, although occasionally the designs run part way down the side in the case of the Algonkian forms. Where decoration has been applied by one of the stamping processes, and more rarely by incision, it is sometimes continued over the lip or rim for an inch or less on the inside. This only occurs in the typical Algonkian forms, and is never seen when incised ornamentation is used. The rims of Iroquoian vessels are never ornamented on the interior, nor is stamping so frequently practised on vessels of this class. The intermediate forms, at least the first of the two mentioned, are frequently ornamented on the interior of the lip. This internal decoration is much more common in the southern portion of this area than elsewhere in the vicinity.

In design, we must of course give up all thought of trying to obtain symbolism, if such there were, for there are no sources now left upon which to base our assumptions. Certain conventional types of decoration seem to have been in vogue, usually consisting in rows of stamped or incised parallel lines and much more rarely of dots regularly arranged in the same manner. Zigzag, chevron, and "herring bone" patterns are the most common, but other angular forms occur, and rows of parallel lines encircling the vessel are sometimes to be found. Stamping and incising as decorative processes never seem to occur on the same vessel. Curvilinear decoration

is exceedingly rare, and not enough material is at hand to show that patterns were used; possibly these were scrolls of some form. On account of the lack of material, it cannot be determined, except in a very general and unsatisfactory way, whether the designs on the Algonkian vessels differ from those on the Iroquoian.

The angle formed where the heavy rim or collar leaves the constricted neck of the Iroquoian vessel is almost invariably notched, and as such collars and angles do not occur on vessels of the true Algonkian type, this feature is necessarily absent from them. It is noticeable that Iroquoian vessels are usually decorated with incised designs, rather than stamped patterns.

 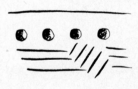

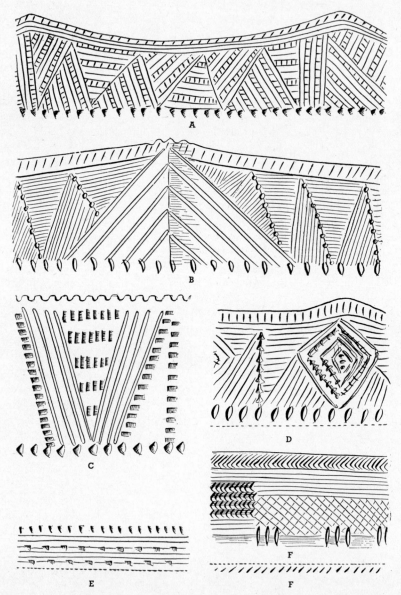

a, *b*, and *d*, designs from Iroquoian vessels; *c*, and *e* designs from an Algonkian vessel; *f*, design from a vessel of the Iroquoian type from a Connecticut rock-shelter, introduced here for comparison.

Pottery is found abundantly on the majority of the sites in this district; but, while very much more common than in the New England area, it does not equal in abundance that from the Iroquois country. It is rarely found buried in graves with skeletons as in the Iroquoian area; when sometimes found in graves, however, it is usually at some distance from the human remains and apparently not connected with them. Whole or nearly whole vessels are exceedingly rare and the number of those found up to date may easily be counted upon the fingers. Potsherds taken from pits or shell-heaps, where they have not been exposed to the action of the weather, are often as thickly covered with grease as when they are broken and cast aside.

ARTICLES OF METAL.

Beads. Beads of native metal, consisting simply of pieces of hammered sheet copper rolled into small tubes, have been found, but they are very rare. Copper salts, but no objects, were found upon the bones, especially on those of the head and neck of a child's skeleton at Burial Ridge, Tottenville, Staten Island, which seemed to indicate the use of copper beads. A great many beads of *olivella* shell, some of them discolored by copper salts, were found about the neck of the skeleton. A single celt of copper is said to have been found in Westchester County, probably on Croton Neck, slightly above the limit of the territory treated in this paper.[1] A large number of copper beads of the type described were found with a skeleton on Constable Hook, Bayonne, New Jersey, and are now in the hands of a private collector in Brooklyn.

ARTICLES OF SHELL.

Wampum. Objects of shell are not at all common, notwithstanding that the coast region of New York was one of the best known localities for wampum manufacture on the continent. Wampum beads are almost unknown from local sites. With the exception of completed beads, most of which may have been taken into the interior, by the Indians, wampum may be found in all stages of manufacture. We refer to the white wampum, for traces of the "black" (blue) wampum made from the hard clam or quahog are so far not reported. The process of manufacture may be shown by shells with the outer whorls broken away in steps until the innermost solid

---

[1] Native copper occurs in the New Jersey trap ridges within a few miles of New York City, an important source in Colonial times being near Boundbrook, 30 miles from the lower end of Manhattan Island. Bowlders of native copper occur in the glacial drift.

column is reached, ground and polished at the end, and needing only cutting off into sections and perforations to make the finished white wampum bead. These do not occur on all sites, though they have been found here and there throughout the region. Ninety-six conch shells with the outer whorls broken entirely away were found in a grave at Burial Ridge, Tottenville, Staten Island, about the head and neck of a skeleton.

Pendants. Occasionally oyster and clam shells, found unworked save for perforations in them, may have been pendants or ornaments, but certainly have little æsthetic value.

Scrapers. Clam shells seem to have been used as scrapers and some are occasionally found with one edge showing the effect of rubbing and wearing. These are rare, however. Some may have been pottery smoothers. Clam shells have been reported which contained central perforations and were identical in appearance with some shell pottery scrapers and smoothers collected by Mr. M. R. Harrington among the Catawba. Contemporary writers mention the use of knives made of shell.

Pottery Tempering. This was sometimes done with calcined and pounded shells, but was uncommon, considering the abundance of the material at hand. Pounded stone or gravel seems to have been more favored.

Pottery Stamps. The corrugated edge of a scallop shell was frequently used as a stamp for pottery, as may be seen by examining the potsherds from this region.

Articles of Bone and Antler.

Objects of bone and antler, while perhaps more abundant here than in New England, are far less plentiful in form and number than in the Iroquoian area. Cut bones are frequent in most shell pits and heaps. They were cut probably with a flint knife, by grooving the bone partly through on all sides, and breaking.

Bone Awls. These utensils are the most common of all bone articles in this region and are found in almost every part of the area. Some are merely sharpened slivers, but others show a considerable degree of work, and are well finished and polished. They are usually made of deer or other mammal bone, but sometimes from the leg bones of birds.

In some instances, the joint of the bone is left for a handle, but this is often cut off. Grooved, perforated, or decorated bone awls are extremely rare in this region. While it is generally considered that these bone tools were used as awls in sewing leather, as by modern shoemakers, nevertheless, they may have served as forks in removing hot morsels from the pot or for a number of other purposes. The latter supposition is supported by the abundance of bone awls found in some shell pits. The Eastern Cree of the Hudson Bay region use a similar bone implement as the catching or striking pin in the cup-and-ball game.

Bone Needles. These are rare, but found in most localities. They are generally made of the curved ribs of mammals and are six or eight inches long, or even longer. They are generally broken across the eye, which is usually midway between the ends. A few with the perforation at one end have been reported.

Bone Arrow Points, usually hollow and conical in shape, have been found, especially at Tottenville, Staten Island, in the Burial Ridge. They are rather rare, but this may be due to the fact that conditions are not suitable for their preservation in most localities. Others are flat and triangular in shape.

Harpoons. No actual barbed bone harpoons, such as occur in the Iroquois country, have been reported from this region; although the writer has seen what appeared to be part of one from Shinnecock Hills, Long Island, whence comes a harpoon barb of bone found by the writer, now in the Museum collection, which was apparently made to tie to a wooden shaft. While neither of these forms seems to occur within this region, several naturally barbed spines from the tail of the sting-ray, found on the Bowman's Brook site, at Mariner's Harbor, Staten Island, may have been used as harpoons or fish spears, for which purpose they were admirably suited by nature. Long, narrow, chipped stone arrowheads are generally called "fish points" but they do not seem peculiarly adapted for this purpose and the name is probably a misnomer. No bone fish hooks are reported from hereabouts, though suggested by early writers.

Bone Beads and Tubes. While so abundant on Iroquoian sites, tubes and beads made of hollow bird or other animal bones, polished and cut in sections, are very rare here.

Draw Shaves, or Beaming Tools, made of bone, and probably used for removing the hair from skins, were made by splitting the bone of a deer's leg, leaving a sharp blade in the middle with the joints on either end as handles. The writer has seen none from this immediate region, but they are reported by Mr. M. R. Harrington. A number were obtained for the Museum by Mr. Ernest Volk in the Lenapé sites near Trenton, New Jersey. An implement, evidently made of the scapula of a deer, and perhaps used as

43

a scraper, was found in a grave at Burial Ridge, Tottenville, Staten Island, by Mr. George H. Pepper.

Worked Teeth. Perforated teeth of the bear, wolf, and other animals, so abundant on Iroquoian sites, never seem to be found here. Beavers' teeth cut and ground to an edge, occur, and may have been used as chisels, or primitive crooked knives, or both, as they were till recently by some of the eastern Canadian Algonkian. Other cut beaver teeth may have served as dice or counters in gaming.

Turtle Shell Cups. These are common, and consist merely of the bony carapace of the box turtle (*Terrapene carolina*), scraped and cleaned inside, the ribs being cut away from the covering to finish the utensil for use.

Antler Implements. Deer antlers and fragments of antler, worked and unworked, occur in all shell-heaps and pits. When whole antlers are found, they usually show at the base the marks of the axe or other implement used to detach them from the skull. Cut antler prongs, prongs broken from the main shaft and others partly hollowed and sharpened show the process of manufacture of antler arrow points. These are characteristic of this area and are usually conical in shape, hollowed to receive the shaft, and with one or more barbs; not infrequently, however, they are diamond-shaped in cross-section. The shaft fitted into the hollow socket as in the case of the conical bone arrow points. A large number were found in and among the bones of human skeletons in a grave at the Burial Ridge, Tottenville, Staten Island.

Cylinders, neatly cut and worked all over, or cylindrical tines made of deer antler cut and rounded only at the ends, are not infrequent, and were probably used as flaking tools in making and finishing arrow points by pressure. One broken cylinder or pin, found on the Bowman's Brook site, Mariner's Harbor, Staten Island, had a rounded, neatly carved head. This specimen, however, seems to be unique.

Pottery Stamps, perhaps of antler or bone but which may be of wood, seem to have been used, judging by the decorations of many pottery sherds. A pottery stamp, carved from antler, was found slightly east of this region, at Dosoris, Glen Cove, Long Island, by Mr. M. R. Harrington, and is now in the Museum collection.

TRADE ARTICLES.

In spite of the frequent mention by old writers of barter of European for Indian goods, the amount of trade material found is small indeed. While it is abundant in the Iroquoian area, all that has ever been found here consists of a few round-socketed iron tomahawks, iron hoes, brass or copper arrow points of various styles, a little porcelain, a few glass beads, Venetian and plain, and some old pipes, notably those stamped "R. Tippet" on the bowl. All these articles are very rare here, and for this no adequate explanation can be given.

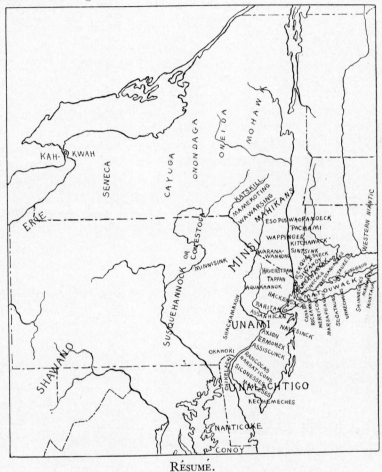

RÉSUMÉ.

The area treated in this paper was inhabited during historic times by the following tribes:[1]

[1]On the map above, these tribes are shown together with the Long Island and other neighboring tribes as indicated by Beauchamp in the map accompanying his "Aboriginal Occupation of New York," New York State Museum, Bulletin 32, Albany, 1900.

A. The Lenni Lenapé, or Delaware, ranging from the Raritan River, including Staten Island, to Saugerties on the west bank of the Hudson.

Raritan or Assanhican.

Hackensack.

Tappan.

Aquakanonk.

Haverstraw.

Waranawankong.

B. The Wappinger Confederacy ranging along the east bank of the Hudson, eastward to Connecticut, from Manhattan Island.

Rechgawawank or Manhattan.

Siwanoy.

Weckquaskeck.

Wappinger.

C. Montauk or Matouwack Confederacy.

Canarsie.

These tribes were surrounded on all sides by neighbors of the same stock, who differed somewhat in their language and culture. On the south and west lay the Lenni Lenapé, or Delaware proper, on the north the Mahikan, and on the east the New England tribes. Almost without exception, these natives were displaced early in the history of this country, and have been long since expatriated or exterminated. A very few mixed bloods may yet be found on Staten Island, Long Island, and in Westchester County, but their percentage of Indian blood is extremely low.

The remains of aboriginal life now to be found consist of shell-heaps, occurring at every convenient point along the coast, on the rivers, and, more rarely, inland; shell, refuse, and fire pits; camp, village, and burial sites; and rock and cave shelters. With one prominent exception,[1] few or no relics have been found in graves. The typical interment was of the flexed variety. Bone burials, also are not infrequent.

Dog skeletons, complete and intact, bearing the appearance of having been laid out, are sometimes found buried in separate graves. Some writers have supposed that these individual dog burials are the remains of "white dog feasts" or kindred practices, because the Iroquois even up to the present day hold such ceremonies. The white dog is entirely cremated by the Iroquois, and so far as we have been able to find out, there is no record of

[1] Burial Ridge, Tottenville, Staten Island.

such occurrences among the Coastal Algonkin; hence, there seems no reason to attribute this custom to them since other Iroquois traits were so infrequent. It seems more probable that such burials are simply those of pet animals, interred as we today honor a faithful dog.

Some of these dog burials may have been sacrifices made to the Underneath Powers, such as horned snakes, just as is the practice of the western Indians today.

In Waessenaer's *Historie Von Europe*, we read of the Mahikan who lived on the Upper Hudson.

It appears that the *Sickanamers* before-mentioned, make a sort of sacrifice. They have a hole in a hill in which they place a kettle full of all sorts of articles that they have, either by them, or procured. When there is a great quantity collected a snake comes in, then they all depart, and the Manittou, that is the Devil, comes in the night and takes the kettle away, according to the statement of the *Koutsinacka,* or Devil hunter, who presides over the ceremony.[1]

* * * * * * *

Our Indians may well have sacrificed dogs and buried them for the mythical snake monsters.

Occasionally, the skeletons of dogs and rarely of other animals have been found in graves associated with human bones. The finding of arrowheads among the ribs of some of these, and other circumstances, seem to point to a practice of killing a favorite animal on the death of its owner to accompany or protect the spirit of its master on the journey to the hereafter.

From their appearance and position, many graves seem to indicate that the dead may sometimes have been buried under the lodge, expecially in winter, when the ground outside was frozen too hard to permit grave digging. Others under the same circumstances seem to have been buried in refuse pits. The remains further indicate that "feasts of the dead" were also held at the time of the interment, judging by the quantity of oyster shells and animal bones in and near the graves. Some graves have rows or layers of oyster shells, with the sharp cutting edge upward, placed above the bodies as if to prevent wild animals from disinterring and devouring the dead.

An interesting fact, brought to light by the rock-shelter work of Messrs. Schrabisch and Harrington in their explorations in New Jersey and in Westchester County, New York is that in the lowest and oldest refuse layers of some of these shelters pottery does not occur. It would be ill advised to

[1]Documentary History of New York, Vol. III, p. 46.

infer from this that the earliest occupants were peoples of another culture from the surrounding village dwellers, as the other artifacts found are quite similar to the implements of the latter. Many reasons for this lack of pottery, such as the more easy transportation of vessels of bark or wood through the mountains and hills, suggest themselves, though they are more or less nullified by the presence of pottery in the upper layers. The upper layer, however, may have been made during the period when the natives were being displaced by Europeans and at the same time subjected to Iroquoian raids, when the villages would naturally be abandoned from time to time, for refuge among the cliffs and caves of the mountain fastnesses.

It has been suggested that the rock and cave shelters are remains of an older occupation by people with or without the same culture as the later known savages. The nature of the finds does not support this view, for the specimens obtained are often of as good workmanship as the best to be found in the villages and cemeteries of the latter, while pottery, on the other hand, occurs on the oldest known Algonkian sites. It seems most probable to the writer that, like the shell-heaps, the rock and cave shelters form but a component part, or phase, of the local culture, perhaps a little specialized from usage and environment, but contemporary with the villages, shell-heaps, and cemeteries of the lowlands.

Mounds and earthworks do not occur in the region under consideration, nor does it appear that most of the Indian villages here were fortified, unless they were slightly stockaded. A number of instances of this are known historically, however, and a few earthworks occur just beyond this area[1].

The remains found do not bear any appearance of very great geological antiquity. In a few instances, rock-shelters, shell-heaps, and village sites seem to possess a relative antiquity; but the oldest known remains, in every case, may be placed as Algonkian with considerable certainty. No paleoliths have been reported, and it would seem from the comparative lack of antiquity of the remains that the natives could not have lived in this region for many centuries before the advent of the whites. The accounts of contemporary writers prove conclusively that these archæological remains, if not those left by Indians found here by the early Dutch and English settlers, must have been from people of very similar culture. In culture, the local Indians were not as high as the Iroquois, nor perhaps as the Lenapé or Delaware proper to whom they are related; but they compare very favorably with the New

[1]An earthwork at Croton Point on the Hudson has been excavated by Mr. M. R. Harrington of the American Museum.

England tribes. Absence and scarcity of certain artifacts, such as steatite vessels, the long stone pestle, the gouge, adze, and plummet, and the abundance and character of bone and pottery articles show them to have been intermediate in character between the Lenapé on the south and west, and the New England tribes on the east and north; and consultations of the old European contemporaries show that this was the case linquistically as well as culturally. Examination of the remains also shows that the influence of the Lenapé on the west, and of the New England peoples on the east, was most strongly felt near their respective borders. Iroquoian influence was strong, as evinced by the pottery, and there is also documentary evidence to this effect. Finally, as is frequent throughout most of eastern North America, the archæological remains may be definitely placed as belonging to the native Indian tribes who held the country at the time of its discovery or to their immediate ancestors.

ABORIGINAL REMAINS ON MANHATTAN ISLAND[1]

THE first field work done on Manhattan Island is of very recent date. Doubtless many articles of Indian manufacture and evidences of Indian occupation were found as the city grew up from its first settlement at Fort Amsterdam, but of these specimens we have very few records. An arrow point found in the plaster on the wall of a Colonial house was, without doubt, in the hands of some member of the Kortrecht family; and Indian pottery has been found in a hut occupied by Hessian soldiers during the War of Independence. The first specimens to have been preserved, to the knowledge of those now interested in the subject, were found in 1855, and consisted of Indian arrow points discovered in Harlem during excavation for a cellar on Avenue A, between 120th and 121st Streets. Some of these are spoken of by James Riker[2] as being in the author's cabinet. Riker also speaks of shell-heaps near here.[3] The next specimens preserved were found at Kingsbridge Road (now Broadway) and 220th Street in 1886, and are in the John Neafie collection at the Museum. These consist of an arrow point and a few bits of pottery. The next work was begun in 1889 by Mr. W. L.

[1]By James K. Finch, revised by Leslie Spier.
[2]History of Harlem (1881), footnote, p. 137.
[3]Ibid., p. 366.

Calver of this city, and has led to the discovery of much valuable material which has been preserved.[1]

The following account of the work is taken mainly from Mr. Calver's notebook:

In the autumn of the year 1889, while exploring the heights of Bloomingdale (now called Cathedral Heights) for any relics that might have remained from the Battle of Harlem, Mr. Calver discovered one arrow point at 118th Street, east of Ninth Avenue, and immediately afterwards a circular hammerstone. On a later trip to the same locality, he found a small grooved axe or tomahawk. In February, 1890, while hunting for Revolutionary relics in the vicinity of Fort Washington, he made a trip to the northern part of the island in search of British regimental buttons, many of which were said to have been found in that vicinity. There he met an old acquaintance, Mr. John Pearce, a policeman then on duty there, by whom he was introduced to Mr. James McGuey, a youth residing in the vicinity of 198th Street and Kingsbridge Road and, while crossing the orchard at Academy Street and Seaman Avenue, Mr. Calver saw that the ground was thickly strewn with shells which afterwards proved to be of Indian origin.

The first Sunday in March, Messrs. Calver and McGuey explored this part of the Island for Indian remains. At the junction of Academy Street and Prescott Avenue, they found an Indian potsherd, the importance of which Mr. McGuey seemed to realize, for, a week later, Mr. Calver met him again and was presented by him with a number of fragments of Indian ware. He assured Mr. Calver that he had found them by digging in an Indian graveyard. The two men dug again at this place, and found more pottery. They then went to Cold Spring, a point on the extreme northern end of the Island, and in a shell-heap there they found more Indian work. Mr. Alexander C. Chenoweth, an engineer then on the Croton Aqueduct, hearing of these discoveries, obtained a permit from the property owners and began to explore "The Knoll" at Dyckman Street and Broadway, for Indian remains. After having finished here, he went to Cold Spring and made some further discoveries. All his specimens were purchased in 1894 by the Museum, and some of them are now on exhibition.

[1]In the Spring of 1890 Mr. Edward Hagaman Hall began his investigations and at about the same time Mr. Reginald Pelham Bolton entered the field of local research. In many instances these gentlemen and Mr. W. L. Calver collaborated with valuable results. In the preservation of the traces of Indian occupation of Manhattan Island the American Scenic and Historic Preservation Society (formed in 1899 under the presidency of the late Hon. Andrew H. Green, but now under that of Dr. George Frederick Kunz) has done much pioneer work.

Since this time, several interesting relics have been found, and as the work of grading streets and other excavation at this part of the Island are carried on, more relics will probably come to light.

The only Indian remains left on the Island, so far as known to the writer, are situated at the extreme northern end at Inwood and Cold Spring. They consist of the so-called shell-heaps or refuse piles from Indian camps, and three rock-shelters at Cold spring. But we have evidence to show that this was not the only part of the Island occupied by the Indians. Mrs. Lamb[1] says that the Dutch found a large shell-heap on the west shore of Fresh Water Pond, a small pond, mostly swamp, which was bounded by the present Bowery, Elm, Canal, and Pearl Streets, and which they named from this circumstance Kalch-Hook. In course of time, this was abbreviated to Kalch or Collect and was applied to the pond itself.[2] This shell-heap must have been the accumulation of quite a village, for Mrs. Jno. K. Van Rensselaer[3] speaks of a castle called Catiemuts overlooking a small pond near Canal Street, and says that the neighborhood was called Shell Point. Hemstreet refers to the same castle as being on a hill "close by the present Chatham Square," and says that it had once been an "Indian lookout."[4] Excavations at Pearl Street are said to have reached old shell banks. "The Memorial History of New York"[5] says that a hill near Chatham Square was called Warpoes, which meant literally a "small hill."[6] According to the same authority, "Corlear's Hoeck was called Naigianac, literally, 'sandlands.' It may, however, have been the name of the Indian village which stood there, and was in temporary occupation." This is the only reference we have to this village, but there are references to another on the lower end of the Island. Janvier[7] says that there was an Indian settlement as late as 1661 at Sappokanican near the present Gansevoort Market. According to Judge Benson,[8] Sappokanican ("tobacco field")[9] was the Indian name for the point afterwards known as Greenwich. "In the Dutch

---

[1]History of New York City, p. 36.

[2]Mr. Edward Hagaman Hall, however, derives the name from "Kolk" or "Kolch," a word still in use in Holland and applied to portions of a canal or inclosure of water.—Editor.

[3]Goede-Vrouw of Manhattan, p. 39.

[4]Hemstreet, Nooks and Corners of Old New York, p. 46.

[5]Bulletin, N. Y. State Museum, Vol. 7, No. 32, p. 107, Feb., 1900.

[6]James G. Wilson, op. cit., p. 52.

[7]Evolution of New York.

[8]N. Y. Historical Society Collections, S. II, Vol. II, Pt. I, p. 84, 1848

[9]All Hilse translations are doubtful.

records references are made to the Indian village of Sappokanican; and this name * * * was applied for more than a century to the region which came to be known as Greenwich in the later, English, times. The Indian village probably was near the site of the present Gansevoort Market; but the name seems to have been applied to the whole region lying between the North River and the stream called the Manetta Water or Bestavaar's Kill."[1] Benton says that the name of the village was Lapinican.[2] Going back to the old Dutch records might lead to finding the actual names and other data regarding these places.

Most of the specimens found on Manhattan Island, as already stated, come from the northern part. We have a few from the central portion, however. There are the arrow-heads spoken of by Riker, and in the Webster Free Library there is a fine specimen of a grooved stone axe found at 77th Street and Avenue B. Mr. Calver has found an arrow-head at 81st Street and Hudson River and specimens from the site of Columbia College have been recorded.

Doubtless the northern part of the Island was inhabited for the longer period; but it is probable that all along the shore, wherever one of the many springs or small brooks, shown on old maps, emptied into the Hudson or East River, there were small, temporary Indian camps. It is likely that these camps were used only in summer, while the primitive occupants of Manhattan retreated to the more protected part of the Island, as at Inwood and Cold Spring, during the winter. Or it may be possible that, as Ruttenber[3] states, the villages on Manhattan Island were only occupied when the Indians were on hunting and fishing excursions, while their permanent villages were on the mainland. Bolton,[4] however, says their principal settlement was on Manhattan Island.

Fort Washington Point. There is a small deposit of shells on the southern edge of the point, in which the writer found some small pieces of pottery and a few flint chips, thus proving its Indian origin. This was probably a summer camp, as it was too exposed for winter use.

Zerren ner's Farm. A favorable sloping field at 194th Street and Broadway now used for truck farming, was utilized as a camp site. Camp débris of varied character has been plowed up here. Perhaps the overhanging

[1]Thos. A. Janvier, in Old New York, pp. 85-86.
[2]New York, p. 26.
[3]Indian Tribes of Hudson's River, p. 78.
[4]History of Westchester County, p. 25.

rocks below Ft. Washington, between 194th and 198th Streets on Bennett Avenue, afforded the Indians some shelter in winter.

Inwood Station Site. At the foot of Dyckman Street and Hudson River, there existed a large deposit of shells, most of which were removed when the rocks on which they lay were blasted away for grading the street. A few arrow points and bits of pottery, as well as several Revolutionary objects, were found here. There are photographs of this deposit in the Museum.

Seaman Avenue Site. This site, between Academy and Hawthorne Streets, running through from Seaman Avenue to Cooper Street, is the most extensive village site from which remains have been collected. It was a British camp site during the Revolution, and a number of buttons, gun-flints, and bullets have been found there, as well as numerous Indian remains. It seems to have been the workshop for a red jasper-like stone of which numerous chips but no finished implements have been found. The shells at this point were first noticed by Mr. Calver in 1890. They may not all be of Indian origin, as some may be due to Revolutionary soldiers.

Harlem River Deposit. Mr. Calver says, "Extending from 209th Street to 211th Street on the west bank of the Harlem River and almost on a line with Ninth Avenue was another large deposit of oyster shells lying just beneath the top soil of the field. These shells had nearly all been disturbed by the plow and were interesting only for their color, which was red. Pieces of horn of deer and split bones of the same animal were common among the shells; but, in spite of the apparent antiquity of the deposit, there were, even in the lowest strata of it, some small fragments of glass, which proved that either the whole mass had been disturbed or else the shells had been left during the historic period." There are several stone sinkers and hammer-stones from this spot in Mr. Calver's collection and at the Museum.

Isham Park Site. On the knolls along the south side of Isham Park, and particularly in Isham's Garden, about on the line of Isham Street and Seaman Avenue, the soil is white with small fragments of shells. A number of arrow points, flint chips, hammerstones, sinkers, and potsherds have been found here. On the knolls to the south of this garden, an Indian burial, shell pockets with small deposits of pottery, etc., and several dog burials, have been found. There are two small shell-heaps, containing chips and potsherds, in the Park on the bank of the Ship Canal, and several shell pockets were disturbed in excavating 218th Street on the north side of the Park.

Cold Spring. Cold Spring is situated at the extreme northern end of Manhattan Island on the southern shore of Spuyten Duyvil Creek. The Indian remains consist of three rock-shelters and three refuse heaps. The rock-shelter is a formation where the overhanging rocks form a small cave or shelter which the Indians used as a dwelling place. All their rubbish, such as oyster shells, broken pottery, and broken arrow-heads, were dumped near by, forming the so-called shell-heaps. Messrs. Calver and McGuey explored the shell-heaps; but Mr. Chenoweth was the first to suspect the existence of the shelters. There is only one which is likely to have been used as a dwelling place, the others being places where food was stored or shelters for fires used in cooking. These shelters face east, and are at the foot of Inwood Hill (formerly called Cock Hill), which forms the most northern part of Manhattan Island. The largest one was formed by several of the rocks breaking off the cliffs above and falling in such a manner that, by digging out some of the earth from beneath them, the Indians could make a small shelter. Probably it was occupied by one family, while the others lived in bark wigwams near by.[1] Another of the shelters is simply an excavation under the end of a huge fragment which also dropped from the cliffs above, and the third is a large crevice in the foot of these cliffs. When Mr. Chenoweth first explored them, all these shelters were completely filled with earth which had gradually worked its way in since their occupation, and much credit is due him for suspecting their presence. In them he found fragments of pottery and stone implements, together with the bones of turkey and deer. The largest of the refuse heaps is situated on a rise directly in front of the shelters. It consists of a layer of shells, in places one foot thick, found under a layer of fine loam, a black earth which has been deposited since the shells were scattered over the original sandy yellow soil. The sheltered position of this place made it an especially desirable camp site. The hills to the south and west formed a protection to the camp from winds, and by Spuyten Duyvil Creek access could be had to either Hudson or East River; while the Cold Spring, from which the place takes its name, furnished an abundant supply of fresh water.

Harlem Ship Canal. Formerly at 220th Street and Kingsbridge Road was a large deposit of shells on the westerly side of the road. This was destroyed when the ship canal was put through. As with the Inwood Station site, no systematic examination of this place was ever made. Mr. John Neafie found some potsherds here in 1886. Mr. Chenoweth also has

[1] Memorial History of New York, Vol. I, p. 33, for picture of houses, and p. 30 for description.

some potsherds from here.[1] Mr. Calver says that this was a large deposit, and that the peculiar thing about it was that the shells were so wedged and packed together that a pick would hardly penetrate them. They lay on the bare rock surface in cracks in the rock; a condition common to this neighborhood.

Shell Pockets at 211th Street. In March, 1903, there was considerable excitement over the reported discovery of an Indian graveyard at 211th Street.[2] The graveyard proved to have been that of some slaves, and was situated on the western end of the rise between 210th and 211th Streets, on the eastern end of which is the old Neagle Burying Ground. This discovery was interesting because under the Negro graves several shell pockets of undoubted Indian origin came to light. The workmen, in grading Tenth Avenue, cut into this hill to obtain material for filling, and uncovered the graves and pockets. It seems almost certain that the deposits were made some time ago; then the wind blew the sand over the deposits to a depth of four or five feet, and Negroes later used this place as a burial ground. In support of this theory is the fact that the pockets were four or five feet under the surface, that the soil above showed no signs of having been disturbed, and that this rise is put down on the Government maps of this section as a sand dune.[3] During the summer of 1904, Mr. Calver with Messrs. Hall and Bolton uncovered nine or more pockets to the southwest of the graveyard.[4] These pockets all seem to have been of the same period as the others, and all appear to have been on the original ground surface, although those farther up the hill were some four feet under the present surface. In one of these pockets was found the complete skeleton of a dog,[5] in another, a turtle shell; two others contained complete snake skeletons; while a fifth held the fragments of a small pottery vessel. The pockets were small, being about three feet in diameter and of equal depth, showing no signs of having first been used as fireplaces and then filled up, though charcoal was scattered among the shells. Almost all the relics from Van Corlandt Park were found by Mr. James in pockets similar to these.

During Indian troubles in 1675, the Wickquaskeek at Ann's Hook, now Pelham Neck, were told "to remove within a fortnight to their usual winter

[1]John Neafie collection, 20-2558; Chenoweth, 20-3498.

[2]Evening Telegram, March 14, 1903.

[3]New York Geologic Folio.

[4]New York Tribune, Oct. 30, 1904, and New York Sun, Dec. 14, 1904.

[5]All that could be saved of this skeleton has been presented to the Museum by Mr. Edward Hagaman Hall.

quarters within Hellgate upon this Island." River says, "This winter retreat was either the woodlands between Harlem Plains and Kingsbridge, at that date still claimed by these Indians as hunting grounds, or Rechawanes and adjoining lands on the Bay of Hellgate, as the words 'within Hellgate' would strictly mean, and which, by the immense shellbeds found there formerly, is proved to have been a favorite Indian resort."[1] A little later the Indians asked to be allowed to return to their maize lands on Manhattan Island and the Governor said that they, "if they desire it, be admitted with their wives and children, to plant upon this Island, but nowhere else, if they remove; and that it be upon the north point of the Island near Spuyten Duyvel."[2]

Mrs. Mary A. Bolton Post, in writing to the editor of "The Evening Post," June 19th of the year of the opening of the Harlem Ship Canal (1895), speaks of some Indians who were allowed to camp on the south side of Spuyten Duyvil Creek on the Bolton property in 1817. Ruttenber says that the Reckgawanc had their principal village at Yonkers, but that on Berrian's Neck (Spuyten Duyvil Hill) was situated their castle or fort called Nipinichsen. This fort was protected by a strong stockade and commanded the romantic scenery of the Papirinimen, or Spuyten Duyvil Creek, and the Mahicanituk (Hudson River), the junction of which as called the Shorackappock. It was from this castle that the Indians came who attacked Hudson on his return down the river.[3] Some small shell deposits occur on Spuyten Duyvil Hill, but as yet this "castile" has not been definitely located. The village site at Yonkers, according to Mr. James, is now covered by buildings; but several relics found near the site years ago are now in the Manor Hall at that place (1904).

Judging from these references, we might conclude that the territory occupied by the tribe commonly known as Manhattan included Manhattan Island and that part of the mainland which is west of the Bronx River south of Yonkers, and that these Indians were a sub-tribe of the Wappinger division of the Mahikan.

Notable Types of Remains.

Dog Burials. The first dog burials were found by Mr. Calver in 1895. The first burial was unearthed at the summit of a ridge of soft earth at 209th Street, near the Harlem River. The ridge, which was about twelve feet

[1]History of Harlem, p. 366.
[2]History of Harlem, p. 369.
[3]Ruttenber, pp. 77-78.

high, had been partly cut away for the grading of Ninth Avenue. It was at the highest part of the hillock that a pocket of oyster and clam shells was noticed, from which a few fragments of Indian pottery which lay on the face of the bank had evidently fallen. The shells, upon inspection, were found to have served as a covering for the skeleton of a dog or wolf. Another burial was found on May 18th within fifty yards of the first burial. It had been covered with shells just as the first one, but had been distributed by workmen. Mr. Calver says: "The two canine burials were situated at a point just without the borders of the Harlem River shell-heap and were distinct from it. The shells were found to be matched, hence it was concluded that they were thrown in unopened or eaten on the spot. As the skeletons were intact and the bones uninjured, all probability of the animals having been eaten is disposed of." These burials are common in this vicinity; Mr. Calver thinks they were for some religious purpose, and suggests a relation to the "White Dog Feast" of the Onondaga of this state.[1] However, it is known that the carcass of the sacrificed dog was burnt by the Iroquois and the explanation given on page 46 is probably correct.

Indian Burials. Notwithstanding all the efforts of various collectors, the first Indian burials to be discovered on the Island were due to the activities of Messrs. Bolton and Calver in 1904. The improvement of Seaman Avenue, Inwood, at that time, uncovered many relics of the long extinct Indian inhabitants, among which Mr. Bolton saw unmistakable signs of Indian graves. To quote from this gentleman: "It thus became evident that there were human interments in the vicinity, and in August, 1907, the first burial was discovered under a shell pit in Corbett's garden. The grading process had been extended only about eighteen inches below the sod, but had sufficed to destroy the jaw of the skeleton which extended upwards, as did also the foot bones. The bones lay in and upon a close mass of oyster shells, some of which were unopened. The skeleton reclined on its right side, facing west. The arms were flexed and crossed, the knees bent and the head thrown back. No traces of weapons were found, nor were there any other objects found, save a fragment of an animal bone.

"The location and position led to further exploration which early in 1908 led to still more interesting discoveries. Sunday, March 22nd, being the first day in the field for exploration for the season for 1908, W. L. Calver and the writer met at Seaman Avenue and Hawthorne Street, Manhattan, to discuss plans for further excavations on this Indian village site. The rains

[1]New York Herald, May 26, 1895.

of the winter 1907-8 had washed the west bank where the layer of oyster shells and black dirt lay along the hill, and a patch of red burnt earth was observed, which on digging out, disclosed a fireplace, evidently of the period of the Revolution, having some large burnt stone, ashes, wood charcoal, brick, broken rum bottles, a wine glass nearly complete, a large open clasp-knife with bone handle, a hoop-iron pot-hook, various forged head nails and

INDIAN BURIAL, MANHATTAN

a curious folding cork-screw. Gold buttons of Revolutionary pattern and an officer's silver button of the Royal Marines, together with pewter buttons of the 17th Regiment, disclosed who had occupied the spot.

"At one part of this fire place, we came upon a pocket of oyster shells, evidently Indian, about two feet deep, and on removing some of these, had the good fortune to uncover a human thigh-bone. We worked carefully into the shells and under the pocket, gradually disclosing the complete remains of a full-grown man lying on its right side, feet to the north, head facing east, knees doubled up, the left arm extended down through the thighs. The feet had been within the area of the hole in which the Revolu-

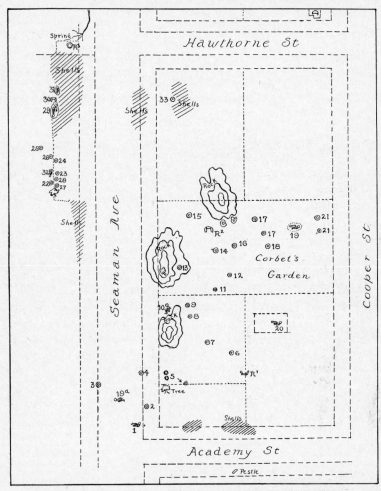

LOCATION OF BURIALS, PITS AND SHELL BEDS NEAR INWOOD

1. Human remains. 2. Shell pit, deer antler. 3. Shell pit. 4. Shell pit, pottery. 5. Shell pits 6. Shell pit, sturgeon below. 7. Shell pit, sturgeon scales. 8, 9. Shell pits. 10. Human remains. 11. Fire pit. 12. Shell pit. 13. Dog burial, puppy. 14. Shell pit. 15. Part of a jar. 16. Shell pit, fish and meat bones. 17. Shell pits. 18. Two dogs in shell pit. 19. Human skeleton, 1907. 19a. Female skeleton, 1908. 20. Human remains when house was built. 21. Small fire pits, Revolutionary. 22. Large shell pit. 23. Large shell pit. 24. Shell pit. 25. Dog burial. 26, 27, 28. Shell pits. 29. Two human skeletons, male and female. 30. Revolutionary fireplace "Royal Marines" and "17th." 31. Skeleton female, and infant. 32. Skeleton (Chenoweth, 1908). 33. Revolutionary fireplace. 71st, officers' buttons. D. Dyckman dwelling. R¹, R². Revolutionary fireplaces. R³. Revolutionary well.

tionary fireplace had been made, and only one or two foot bones were found. At a later period other foot bones were found on the opposite side of the Revolutionary fireplace, evidently having been displaced in its construction. The right arm was flexed, and the hand was under the head, the latter was intact and every tooth was in place. Shells had been packed over the body, and some around it. We were much puzzled by a number of human bones lying compactly together by the skeleton, in a position that would have been in its lap, had it been upright.

"We removed the skull, covered the remains, and on Sunday, March 29th, renewed the work. We went carefully to work upon the cluster of mixed bones in front of the large skeleton, and soon found them to be rather compactly arranged in a rectangular form about 14 by 26 inches, the long bones parallel. The vertebræ ended abruptly parallel with the head of the larger skeleton, and after working some time, we found a skull placed below, beneath the pile of bones in a vertical position, facing north, the lower jaw of which was disengaged, and was placed sideways in front of the face. The back of the skull was broken in, and was black with marks of burning. The lower jaw was burned, and some of the teeth split by fire. The arm and leg bones were charred at the joints. Inside the skull was a burned toe bone. There were some oyster shells among the charred remains.

"A significant fact was that the right arm bones of the large skeleton were below the pile of burned bones. This feature, and the compact arrangement of the latter within the space in front of and at the same level as the large skeleton, seem to point strongly towards an intentional arrangement of these bones, in front of the large corpse and to indicate the simultaneous burial of the two bodies. On examination, the large skeleton proved to be that of an adult male, and the dismembered remains those of a female of about 35 years of age. No implements were found with the remains, but a part of a stone pestle and a rude celt lay under the sod among the oysters above the large skeleton.

"On Sunday, June 14, 1908, another burial was found about 20 feet north of the above. This burial consisted of an adult skeleton doubled up and its back much curved, and was apparently that of a female of mature age. Between the knees, the remains of a small infant were laid, the skull of the latter being fragmentary. The right hand of the adult was below the infant and the left hand around the throat. The skull was intact and had nearly all the teeth. One finger bone had grown together at the joint in a crooked position apparently due to disease. On lifting the ribs of the right side, an arrow-head of flint fell out between the fourth and fifth bones. These skeletons lay about two and a half feet below the grass, and a pocket of oyster shells was over the heads. The woman's remains lay within a space about 31 inches long by 50 inches wide, flat in the hard red sand bed facing east.

"Shortly after these remains were discovered, Mr Chenoweth extended the excavation previously made by the explorers at the side of a large oyster shell pit in the same bank of sand, and uncovered a male skeleton of which he preserved the skull. Some small fragments of the skeleton were afterwards found by the writer on this spot. Contractors for the sewer in Seaman Avenue also uncovered the remains of a young female close to the position of several of the shell pits previously described. These interments have some curious features. The position of the remains facing east, sometimes west, the absence of weapons or other objects and the oyster shells packed with or above them are subjects for interesting discussion on which future finds may throw much light, as also upon the peculiar double burial and the burnt state of the female remains."

BIBLIOGRAPHY.

Anthropological Papers of the American Museum of Natural History, Volume III; Hudson-Fulton Publication, "The Indians of Greater New York and the Lower Hudson." New York, 1909.

This volume contains a series of papers by Messrs. Finch, Bolton, Harrington, Speck, Schrabisch, and Skinner, dealing minutely with all phases of the subject in a thoroughly scientific and less popular manner than the present volume. Especial attention is paid to the research in local archæology, with maps and notes on most of the important sites. The Museum also published a guide leaflet to the collection on exhibition.

Skinner, Alanson, The Indians of Greater New York. Torch Press, Cedar Rapids, Iowa, 1915.

A very full and thoroughgoing account of the history and ethnology of the local Indians, containing many sources not available at the time when Volume III of the Anthropological Papers was published. The archæology of the locality is also written up in a more popular style than the preceding publication. These two papers with the present guide leaflet bring the subject of our local Indians thoroughly up to date and summarize the older authors.

Ruttenber, E. M., History of the Indian Tribes of the Hudson River. Albany, 1872.

A little old-fashioned in style, and with a few errors, but brimful of all sorts of useful information on the subject.

Beauchamp, Rev. W. M., Bulletin of the New York State Museum. Nos. 16, 18, 22, 32, 41.

These list, figure, and described the types of chipped and polished stone implements, and the pottery, shell, bone, metal, and wooden utensils found in New York State. Bulletin 32 contains a list of all the Indian village and camp sites, shell-heaps, rock and cave shelters, and cemeteries then recorded from the entire state, with a map upon which the locations of these are plotted. This series is invaluable to the student, especially to one engaged in research work.

Farrand, Livingston, Basis of American History. Harpers: The American Nation Series, Vol. I.

"This volume contains a careful review of the physical features of North America, which is exceedingly helpful to the student in understanding the development of the various colonies. This is supplemented by a survey of the principal lines of communication—Indian trails, portages, water-ways, and mountain passes—which have been of the utmost importance in determining the course of events in American history * * * Of particular value is Professor Ferrand's able discussion of the American Indians. Reasoning from a great mass of collected data, he reaches sane and conservative conclusions. The author has made a point of condensation, and has supplied the want of a thorough, systematic study of the Indians in a small compass."

Heckewelder, J. G. E., History, Manners, and Customs of the Indian Nations who once inhabited Pennsylvania. Philadelphia, 1876.

At the present writing this is the most complete source of information on the Delaware Indians from the time of their migration from New Jersey and Eastern Pennsylvania to the Ohio Valley.

Harrington, M. R., Some Customs of the Delaware Indians, the Museum Journal of the Museum of the University of Pennsylvania, Vol. I, No. 3; and Vestiges of Material Culture Among the Canadian Delawares, American Anthropologist, N. S., Vol. 10, No. 3, 1908; A Preliminary Sketch of Lenapé Culture, Ibid, Vol. 15, p. 208.

The most recent account of the Delaware, but merely preliminary sketches, forerunners of a much larger work based on personal archæological research about New York City and ethnological study among the surviving Delaware of Canada and Oklahoma, which, when given to the public, will be the *dernier mot* on the subject.

Brinton, D. G., The Lenapé and Their Legends. Philadelphia, 1885.

This work contains the Walum Olum and its translation, in addition to a mass of ethnological material. An excellent treatise on the Delaware Indians.

O'Callaghan, E. B., Documentary History of New York. Four volumes. Albany, 1863-7.

Contains, as its name implies, many of the early documents relating to the settlement of New York. A very important work containing many of the sources of the present volume.

De Vries, David Peterson, Voyages from Holland to America; (translation). New York 1853.

A rare and valuable work, to be obtained only in the large public libraries. This is the personal account of the good patron's own experience as an eye-witness and participator in the early Indian wars in the New Netherlands. Written in a naive, fluent, and interesting manner.

Morgan, Lewis H., The League of the Iroquois. In several editions.

A comprehensive study of the Five, later Six Nations, especially of the Seneca. One of the first careful scientific studies ever made of any tribe, and still a classic.

Parker, A. C., An Erie Indian Village and Cemetery; Iroquois Corn Foods; and other publications in the Bulletins of the New York State Museum, Albany, N. Y.; in the same series as those of Dr. William Beauchamp.

The first of the works mentioned is the best published account of the archæological work on any one site in the state, and should be read by everyone intending to do research.

The second gives a valuable insight into ancient Indian methods of cookery.

All of Mr. Parker's works are valuable because of his deep knowledge of all things Indian and his experience as State Archæologist.

Furman, Gabriel, Antiquities of Long Island. New York, 1874.

Tooker, W. W., Indian Place-Names on Long Island. New York, 1911. (Knickerbocker Press).

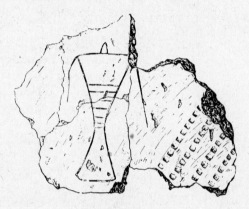

THE THUNDERBIRD

Engraved on a fragment of pottery found at Shinnecock Hills, Long Island. The thunderbirds were gods and patrons or warriors and it is one of their duties to guard mankind from the evil horned serpents (page 10) that dwell under the earth or beneath the waters.